Spelling Thinkercises

by
Becky Daniel

illustrated by Nancee McClure

Cover by Nancee McClure

Copyright © Good Apple, Inc., 1988

ISBN No. 0-86653-423-7

Printing No. 987654321

**GOOD APPLE, INC.
BOX 299
CARTHAGE, IL 62321-0299**

The purchase of this book entitles the buyer to reproduce student activity pages for classroom use only. Any other use requires written permission from Good Apple, Inc.

All rights reserved. Printed in the United States of America.

Dedication

For my late grandfather, Frank Knight, who always made me feel special.

Table of Contents

BUILDING WORDS
- Word Wheels 1
- Word Diamonds 2
- Little Words 3
- Something's Missing 4
- Fill-Ins 5
- Missing Consonants and Vowels 6
- Safe Additives 7
- Add Two or Three 8
- S.W. and S.T.R. 9
- Vowels and Consonants Needed 10
- Alphabet Sentences 11
- Missing and Extra Letters 12

RHYMING WORDS
- Great, Grand and Clue 13
- Day and Grade 14
- Dynamite and Giraffes 15
- Lightweight Rhymes 16
- Rhyme Time 17

SYNONYMS
- Synonym Search 18
- Synonyms, Synonyms 19
- Synonym Roundup 20
- Synonym Puzzles 21
- Synonyms, Please 22
- Synonyms Galore 23
- Synonym Acrostics 24
- More Synonym Acrostics 25
- Imaginary Synonyms 26
- Synonym Parts 27
- Synonym Scramble 28
- Synonym Review 29

ANTONYMS AND HOMONYMS
- Antonyms Plenty 30
- Antonyms Anyone? 31
- Synthetic Antonyms 32
- Neat and Rough 33
- Homonyms, Homonyms 34
- More Homonyms 35

SPELLING BOGGLERS
- Animal, Vegetable or Mineral? 36
- Whatch-A-Ma-Call-Its 37
- Mind Bogglers 38
- More Bogglers 39
- It Can Be Done! 40
- Hide and Seek Spelling 41
- You Decide 42
- Weeding Words 43
- Can You Spell? 44
- Eight Great ATEs 45
- Word Chains 46
- More Word Chains 47
- Complete Sentences 48

MYSTERY WORD BOGGLERS
- More Mystery Word Fun 49
- Perfect Word Squares 50
- Mystery Word Magic 51
- Ten-Letter Words 52
- Mystery Word Zoo 53
- Palindromes 54
- Spelling Puns 55

ANSWER KEY 56

AWARD CERTIFICATES 59

To the Teacher

Spelling Thinkercises is designed to give students' minds a real workout! Children will learn the spellings and meanings of hundreds of new words when they tackle these exciting and motivating spelling puzzles. The wide range of activities, from simple to complex, gives learners concrete practice in spelling and using new words.

Most children are involved in spelling programs based on memorizing words rather than building vocabulary skills. The activities in this book require children to THINK, use their imaginations and dictionaries while learning to spell, alphabetize and categorize new words. The complexity of most of the activities makes dictionary work a must, and children should be encouraged to use their dictionaries while completing the spelling activities.

Each page contains a bonus. These activities are usually very difficult and should not be a requirement. Use these activities for extra credit. Students that complete one of these should receive special recognition. A class competition could involve keeping track of how many bonuses are completed by each student and rewarding those that complete a given number. Awards are found on pages 59 and 60 and a special award certificate for bonuses is included.

An answer key is provided; however, since very often the puzzles are open-ended, the answer key will provide only a list of possible answers. For many activity pages, learners will have their own unique lists of answers. Discussion of alternative answers should be encouraged. If time allows, have the children follow up each activity page by creating their own puzzles.

Word Wheels

Place a letter in each empty space so that the letters spell words moving from the outside to the center. List the eight words below each ring. There is more than one possible answer for each puzzle.

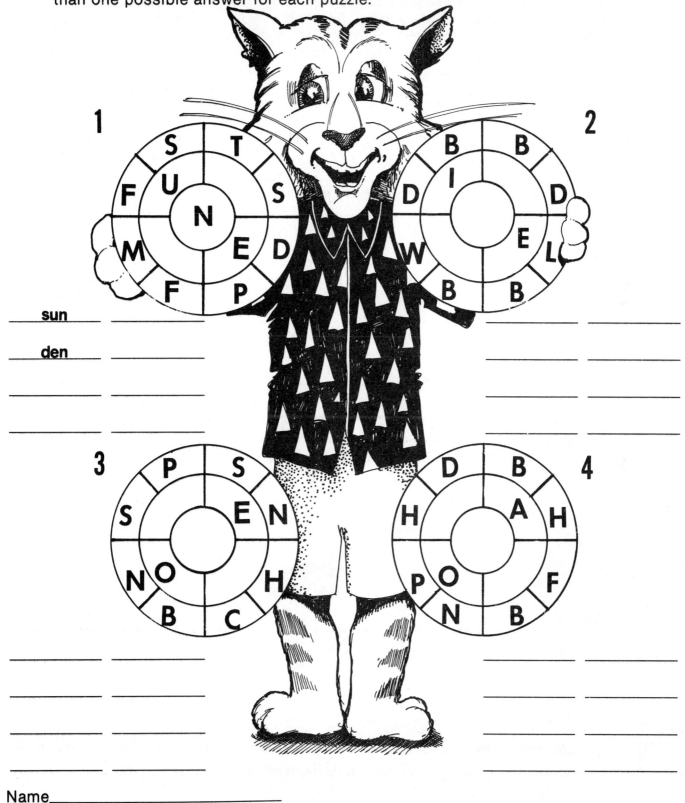

sun

den

Bonus: Make your own word ring using some of your favorite words.

Word Diamonds

A word diamond has thirteen letters and six words. The six words read down and across. Complete these word diamonds. You must use six different words in each diamond. Then create a word diamond of your own in the last space.

Example:

```
    F
   CAT
  BACON
   BET
    S
```

1.
```
    M
   _A_
  __K___
   _E_
    S
```

2.
```
    L
   ___
  B___S
   ___
    S
```

3.
```
    _
   ___
  _____
   ___
    _
```

Bonus: Make your own word diamond using only the names of people.

Example:
```
    S
   JUD
  JASON
   NAN
    N
```

Name_____

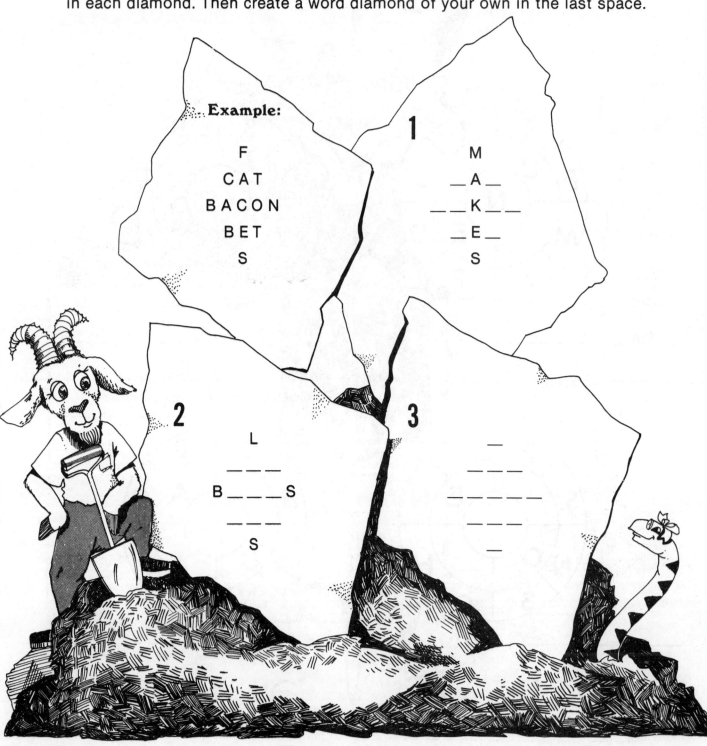

Little Words

1. Add a three-letter word to the letters below to form bigger words.

   S _ _ _ K

   P _ _ _ Y

   B _ _ _ S

   B _ _ _ S

   T _ _ _ B

   B _ _ _ D

   S _ _ _ E

   T _ _ _ K

   H _ _ _ Y

2. Add a four-letter word to the letters below to form bigger words.

   T _ _ _ _ S

   T _ _ _ _ S

   T _ _ _ _ S

   C _ _ _ _ S

Name _____

Bonus: What should you always take when you go dancing? The mystery word doesn't contain any of the vowels *a, e, i, o* or *u*.

_____

3

Something's Missing

"NOPE"

ch ___
gall ___
gr ___
sc ___
pl ___

1. The same three-letter word can be added to each group of letters above to spell new words.

2. Fill in the spaces with letters to spell words that fit the clues.

   edge of a cup

   ___ i ___

   edge of patience

   ___ ___ i ___ ___

   edge of California

   ___ ___ ___ i ___ ___

   line that edges

   ___ ___ ___ ___ i ___ ___

3. Fill in the blanks with consonants to spell a list of eight tools.

   ___ i ___ e
   ___ a ___ ___ e ___
   ___ i ___ e
   ___ ___ i e ___
   ___ ___ i
   ___ ___ i ___ o ___ ___
   ___ ___ o ___ a ___ o ___
   ___ ___ e ___ ___ i ___ e ___

4. Each word below is missing the same letter two or more times. Fill in the blanks to spell a list of eight machines.

   l ___ v ___ r
   w h ___ ___ l
   p u ___ ___ e y
   d e ___ ___ i c k
   f ___ l c r ___ m
   r u ___ ___ e r
   c ___ o w b a ___
   w ___ d g ___

Name _____

Bonus: Use the eight tools and eight machines you listed in numbers 3 and 4 to create a word search for a friend.

Fill-Ins

1. Fill in the blanks to spell five synonyms for the word *up-to-date*.

c u r r e n t

c o _ _ e _ _

o n t _ _ _ _ _ _ _

t e m _ _ _ _ _

p o _ _ _ _ _ _

o r a _ _ _ _ _

r y _ _ _ _ _

2. Fill in the blanks with letters to spell words that fit the clues.

obtain   _ e _

results   _ _ e _ _

get   _ _ _ e _ _ _

give   _ _ _ e _ _ _

3. Fill in the blanks below to spell words with double consonants in the middle.

_ _ l l _ _ _

_ _ b b _ _

_ _ g g _ _ _

4. One two-letter combination will complete each word below. What letter combination will make all three spell a word?

g u i t _ _

c a v i _ _

s t _ _

Name _____

Bonus: What four-letter word means a particle, a bit, a fragment and a chunk?

_ _ _ _

5

Missing Consonants and Vowels

1. The sentences below have some missing vowels. Can you spell words by filling in the missing vowels to form sentences?

   T___ h___v___ fr___ ___nds, b___ ___ fr___ ___nd.

   Y ___ c ___ n l ___ ___rn fr ___ m ___ v ___ ry p ___ rs ___ n y ___ ___ m ___ ___ t.

   L ___ k ___ y ___ ___ rs ___ lf ___ nd ___ th ___ rs w ___ ll l ___ k ___ y ___ ___ t ___ ___ .

2. The sentences below have some missing consonants. Can you spell words by filling in the blanks to form sentences?

   ___ ___e ___i___e ___o ___e happy i___ ___ow.

   A happy ___ie___ i___ ___i___e a jolly ___o___ ___.

Name _____

Bonus: Rearrange the letters found below to spell a day of the week.

aaoeeedfwkyth _____

6

Safe Additives

Each sentence found below has words with double letters. The second double letter is missing in some of the words. Add the correct letters to the words to spell complete sentences.

I ned a spon to eat my puding.
_____

She is to we to reach the fidle.
_____

A rabit ran acros the gras to fast to se.
_____

A bal wil rol downhil.
_____

Thre tres wil freze when slet fals.
_____

Name _____

Bonus: What ten-letter word means to leap, head over heals and turn?

Add Two or Three

1. Add girls' names to the beginning of the letters listed below to form words.

_ _ _ e r a g e

_ _ _ _ t i c

_ _ i n

_ _ _ b e

_ _ _ _ _ -corner

_ _ _ i e n c e

_ _ _ _ _ t m a s

_ _ _ a r d

2. Can you spell five, four-letter words that begin with the letter *c* and end with the letter *w*?

c _ _ w

c _ _ w

c _ _ w

c _ _ w

c _ _ w

3. A three-letter combination will complete each word below. What three-letter combination will work in all three words?

s t _ _ _

g i r _ _ _ e

c h _ _ _

4. Add the name of a three-letter animal to the beginning of the letters listed below to form words.

_ _ _ c h u p

_ _ _ m e n t

_ _ _ a r d

_ _ _ g y

_ _ _ i n g

_ _ _ x

_ _ _ f

Name _____

Bonus: What do these four words have in common?
embarassed   wierd   untill   seperate

S.W. and S.T.R.

1. Many words that begin with the letters *sw* suggest a sudden turn, spin or dizziness. Can you spell twelve words that begin with *sw* and suggest turning, spinning, dizziness or quick movement?

   1. _____
   2. _____
   3. _____
   4. _____
   5. _____
   6. _____
   7. _____
   8. _____
   9. _____
   10. _____
   11. _____
   12. _____

2. Many words that begin with the letters *str* suggest a motion or an exertion. Can you spell eighteen words beginning with *str* that suggest a motion or exertion?

   1. _____
   2. _____
   3. _____
   4. _____
   5. _____
   6. _____
   7. _____
   8. _____
   9. _____
   10. _____
   11. _____
   12. _____
   13. _____
   14. _____
   15. _____
   16. _____
   17. _____
   18. _____

Name _____

Bonus: Add five letters to the word *light* to make a word that means pleasant.

Vowels and Consonants Needed

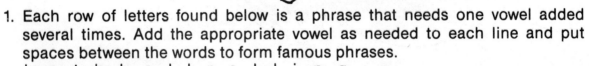

1. Each row of letters found below is a phrase that needs one vowel added several times. Add the appropriate vowel as needed to each line and put spaces between the words to form famous phrases.

   k p t h b a l l r o l l i n g
   keep the ball rolling

   t h r o u g h t h c k a n d t h n
   _____

   w h l e k i t a n d c a b d l e
   _____

   p a i n t t h t o w n r d
   _____

   n t h e n c k o f t m e
   _____

   k n w t h e r p e s
   _____

   u t n a l i m b
   _____

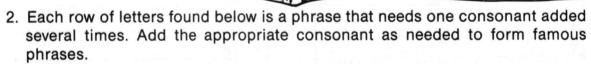

2. Each row of letters found below is a phrase that needs one consonant added several times. Add the appropriate consonant as needed to form famous phrases.

   h o s e o f a n o t h e c o l o
   horse _____

   a a x t o g r i d
   _____

   r a i c a t s a d d o g s
   _____

   u s e t t h e a l e c a r t
   _____

   o a l k u r k e y
   _____

   l e h e c a o u o f h e b a g
   _____

Name _____

Bonus: What five-letter animal begins with double ll's?

10

Alphabet Sentences

Write a sentence for each letter of the alphabet. Each sentence must contain an adjective, a noun and a verb beginning with the appropriate letter.

Example: B = A *beautiful baboon baked bread.*

a_____
b_____
c_____
d_____
e_____
f_____
g_____
h_____
i_____
j_____
k_____
l_____
m_____
n_____
o_____
p_____
q_____
r_____
s_____
t_____
u_____
v_____
w_____
x_____
y_____
z_____

Name _____

Bonus: Write a story in which the first letter of each word is alphabetized.
Example: **A**bby **b**akes **c**akes. **D**on **e**ats **f**ive.

Missing and Extra Letters

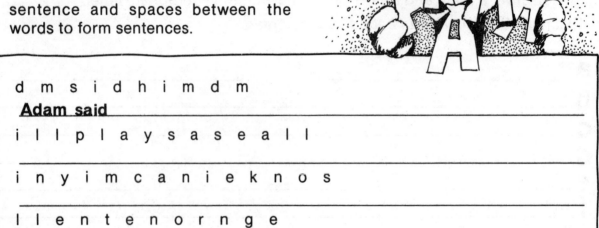

1. The letters below are sentences with the same letter missing more than once. Put the missing letters in each sentence and spaces between the words to form sentences.

   d m s i d h i m d m
   Adam said
   _____

   i l l p l a y s a s e a l l
   _____

   i n y i m c a n i e k n o s
   _____

   l l e n t e n o r n g e
   _____

2. In each sentence found below, some extra letters have been added. Cross out the extra letters and spell words to form sentences.

   It ~~h~~is too~~k~~ late to seem there movie.
   It is
   _____

   It saw an bug ton them flower.
   _____

   Herre twoday, goonee topmooerrow.
   _____

3. Cross out five letters in each line to spell four, seven-letter words.

   v e ~~x~~ h e i c y c l e t
   v **e** **h** __ __ __ __

   b e d c a p u z z l e d
   __ __ __ __ __ __ __

   d e o l l p i h e i n e
   __ __ __ __ __ __ __

   g o t o e u b l a e s h
   __ __ __ __ __ __ __

Name _____

Bonus: Use the four, seven-letter answers in number 3 to create a sentence. Your sentence must make sense.

Great, Grand and Clue

1. Spell a word that rhymes with the word *great* for each letter of the alphabet listed below.

   a **ate**   l ___
   b ___   m ___
   c ___   n ___
   d ___   p ___
   e ___   r ___
   f ___   s ___
   g ___   t ___
   h ___   v ___
   i ___   w ___

2. Fill in each blank with a consonant to spell six words that rhyme with the word *and*.

   g __ a n __
   g __ a n __
   __ o m m a n __
   __ i t h __ a n __
   u __ d e r __ a n __
   e x __ a __

3. Write a word that rhymes with the word *clue* for each clue found below.

   a farewell ___ ___ **i** **e** **u**

   crooked **a** **s** ___ ___ ___

   first public appearance ___ ___ **b** **u** **t**

   a meeting to seek information
   ___ ___ ___ ___ ___ **i** **e** **w**

Name _____

Bonus: Can you spell an antonym for the word *award* that rhymes with *grand*?

___ ___ ___ ___ ___ ___ ___

Day and Grade

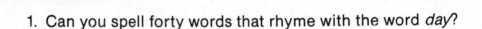

1. Can you spell forty words that rhyme with the word *day*?

1. **array**	11. _____	21. _____	31. _____
2. _____	12. _____	22. _____	32. _____
3. _____	13. _____	23. _____	33. _____
4. _____	14. _____	24. _____	34. _____
5. _____	15. _____	25. _____	35. _____
6. _____	16. _____	26. _____	36. _____
7. _____	17. _____	27. _____	37. _____
8. _____	18. _____	28. _____	38. _____
9. _____	19. _____	29. _____	39. _____
10. _____	20. _____	30. _____	40. _____

2. Fill in each blank with a vowel to correctly spell eight words that rhyme with the word *grade*.

st __ ck __ d __   __ rc __ d __

t __ r __ d __   m __ rm __ l __ d __

c __ sc __ d __   m __ sq __ __ r __ d __

s __ __ d __   ch __ r __ d __

Name _____

Bonus: What is the longest list of rhyming words you can spell? Can you make a list with thirty words? Forty? Fifty?

Dynamite and Giraffes

1. Can you spell thirty-five words that rhyme with the word *dynamite*?

1. _____	10. _____	19. _____	28. _____
2. _____	11. _____	20. _____	29. _____
3. _____	12. _____	21. _____	30. _____
4. _____	13. _____	22. _____	31. _____
5. _____	14. _____	23. _____	32. _____
6. _____	15. _____	24. _____	33. _____
7. _____	16. _____	25. _____	34. _____
8. _____	17. _____	26. _____	35. _____
9. _____	18. _____	27. _____	

2. Cross out the extra letters in each row and spell words that rhyme with the word *giraffe*.

p r̸ h ȟ o t o e g e r a p h y
p **h** **o** _ _ _ _ _ _

p e a r i n a g e r a p h e s
_ _ _ _ _ _ _ _ _ _

e x t p h o n o g r a p h i n g
_ _ _ _ _ _ _ _ _

s e n t e l a e g r
_ _ _ _ _ _ _

e a p h r
_ _ _ _

Name _____

Bonus: Can you spell a color that doesn't rhyme with any other words?

15

Lightweight Rhymes

1. What five-letter word will complete each word found below?

   fl _ _ _ _ _
   b _ _ _ _ _
   p _ _ _ _ _
   ann _ _ _ _ _
   pron _ _ _ _ _

2. Can you spell eight, five-letter words that rhyme with *back*?

   _ _ack   _ _ack
   _ _ack   _ _ack
   _ _ack   _ _ack
   _ _ack   _ _ack

3. Can you spell a word that rhymes with the word *ice* for each clue found below?

   cinnamon _ _ _ _ _
   cost _ _ _ _ _
   cut _ _ _ _
   shake and roll _ _ _ _
   more than once _ _ _ _ _
   food _ _ _ _
   opinion given _ _ _ _ _
   _ _ _ _ louse _ _ _ _

4. Find and circle sixteen words that rhyme with the word *ace* hidden in the letter maze.

b	a	s	e	b	f	a	c	e	g
g	r	s	i	r	p	a	c	e	r
r	a	p	c	a	s	e	t	r	i
a	c	a	h	c	l	p	r	e	m
c	e	c	a	e	a	l	a	p	a
e	i	e	s	a	c	a	c	l	c
v	a	s	e	c	e	c	e	a	e
e	r	a	s	e	a	e	c	c	a
a	c	r	e	t	r	a	c	e	x

Name _____

Bonus: Use the eight words that rhyme with *back* in number 2 to create a crossword puzzle.

16

Rhyme Time

1. Use all the letters listed to complete three rhyming words. You may not use a letter more than once unless it is listed more than once. One word is the name of an animal, one is a flower.

   a c̶ e e h h̶ i l l n o̶ o̶ o r s̶ t t

   <u>h o r o s c</u> ope

   _ _ _ _ _ _ _ ope

   _ _ _ _ _ ope

2. Use all the letters listed below to complete three rhyming words. Cross out each letter after you use it.

   a a b̶ c̶ l l r t t̶ y p h

   <u>c</u> _ _ _ _ oon

   <u>t</u> _ _ _ _ oon

   <u>b</u> _ _ _ oon

An animal and a flower that end in "ope"???

3. Spell a word that rhymes with the word *speak* for each clue found below.

   to evaluate <u>**critique**</u>

   mild tempered _____

   depressing _____

   part of the face _____

   much like an onion _____

   to search _____

   old and valuable _____

4. Start in any circle. Move along circles connected by a line. Stop at any letter. Can you spell eight words that rhyme with the letters *aint*?

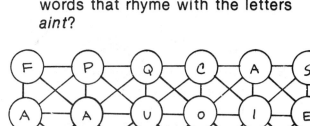

<u>**faint**</u> _____   _____

_____   _____

_____   _____

_____   _____

Name _____

Bonus: What is the longest sentence you can write in which every word rhymes? Example: I fly high.

Synonym Search

1. Add vowels to complete the spellings of five synonyms for the word *instrument*.

   t __ __ l
   __ m p l __ m __ n t
   d __ v __ c __
   __ t __ n s __ l
   __ p p l __ __ n c __

2. Every vowel found in the words listed below is incorrect. Change incorrect vowels to spell synonyms for the word *spot*.

   merk _____
   spuck _____
   smadgu _____
   steun _____
   blatch _____
   blit _____
   blamosh _____

3. Can you spell four synonyms for the word *predict*? Each word must begin with the four-letter word *fore*.

   fore _____
   fore _____
   fore _____
   fore _____

Bonus: Unscramble the words found below to discover some hints about the mystery word.

tgypEian _____
loisd fgiuer _____
posling dsies _____
Mystery Word: __ y __ __ __ i __

Name _____

Synonyms, Synonyms

1. What five letters in the word *blossom* spell a synonym for blossom?
   _____
   What four letters in the word *regulate* spell a synonym for regulate?
   _____
   What two letters in the word *exist* spell a synonym for exist?
   _____
   What four letters in the word *masculine* spell a synonym for masculine?
   _____

2. Hidden among the letters in each row are two synonyms. Find and circle the two synonyms in each row of letters.

   (same)andidenticalifix
   dogshowexdisplaysold
   gosleepeepresteating

3. Circle the synonym for the first word found in each row.

tie	sever	(tether)	loosen
honor	dishonor	deceit	integrity
perplex	waffle	baffle	clarify
conquer	rout	submit	surrender
break	fracture	mend	unite
gallantry	valor	cowardice	timidity
adore	beautiful	exalt	dislike
duplicate	imitation	accurate	original

Name _____

Bonus: Write a synonym for eight uncircled words in number 3.

Synonym Roundup

1. Can you find and circle a synonym for the word *wander* hidden in each line of letters? The letters are in order, but extra letters have been added.

   r(o)b o l w(v)(e) y e n o t   **rove**
   r e d g r e e n o a e m b   _____
   m e n r a m b o o l e e k   _____
   m e a t n o d e e r b o t   _____
   d r o s e i f e e t o e x   _____
   s o u t r e w a x t y p u   _____

2. Can you find and circle ten synonyms for the word *decrease* hidden in the letter maze?

   (d i m i n i s h) e s
   i w s h o r t e n u
   v l i b i e o d s b
   i e c n d n r e h t
   d s c u d d t f r r
   e s a t t l o l i a
   r e d u c e e a n c
   g n d e f l a t k t
   a b b r e v i a t e

3. Can you spell two synonyms for the word *secure* that fit in the puzzle found below?

   (cross puzzle with letters s at top, s-a across)

Bonus: Can you spell two synonyms for the word *believe* with the appropriate number of letters to fit in the puzzle found below.

(cross puzzle with letter i)

Name _____

20

Synonym Puzzles

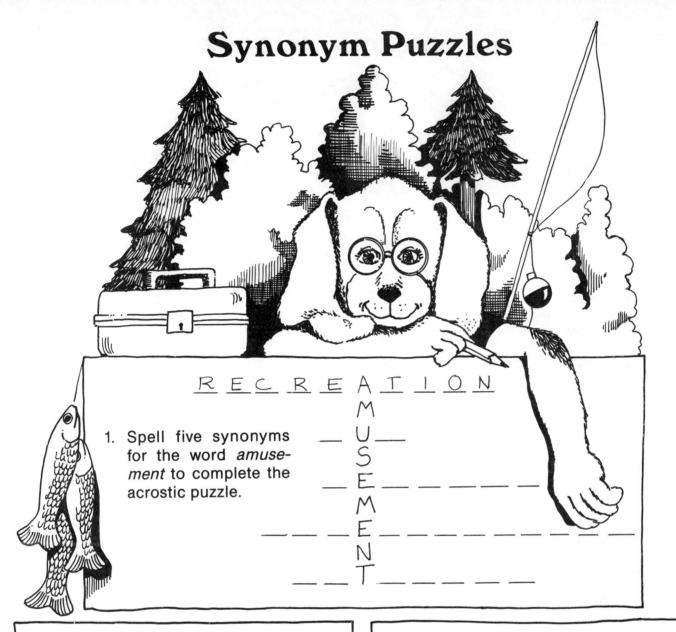

1. Spell five synonyms for the word *amusement* to complete the acrostic puzzle.

   R E C R E A T I O N
   _ _ _ A _ _ _ _
   _ _ M _ _ _ _ _
   _ _ _ U _ _ _ _
   _ _ _ S _ _ _ _
   _ _ _ E _ _ _ _
   _ _ M _ _ _ _ _
   _ _ E _ _ _ _ _
   _ _ N _ _ _ _ _
   _ _ T _ _ _ _ _

2. In each line is hidden a synonym for the word *shining.* The letters are in the correct order, but extra letters have been added.

   r e a d d i s a n t v o **radiant**
   l e u i s a t r o e u s e _____
   s t p a e r k e y l i n g _____
   s t e a w i n e k l i n g _____
   g l e a i m m t e r i n g _____

3. Add vowels to complete the spellings of five synonyms for the word *inspection*.

   _ n q _ _ r y
   _ n v _ s t _ g _ t _ _ n
   p r _ b _
   s c r _ t _ n y
   _ x _ m _ n _ t _ _ n
   c h _ c k _ p

Name _____

Bonus: What synonym for the word *stone* means to sway from side to side?

_ _ _ _

21

Synonyms, Please

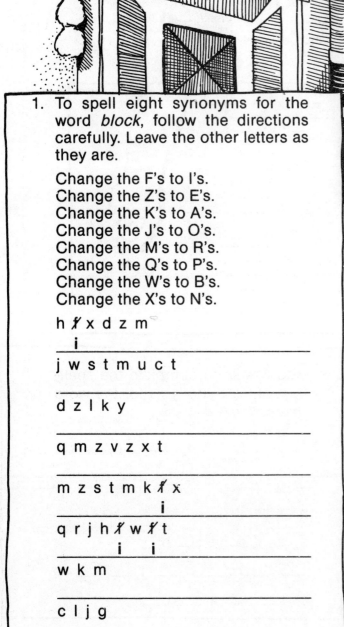

1. To spell eight synonyms for the word *block*, follow the directions carefully. Leave the other letters as they are.

   Change the F's to I's.
   Change the Z's to E's.
   Change the K's to A's.
   Change the J's to O's.
   Change the M's to R's.
   Change the Q's to P's.
   Change the W's to B's.
   Change the X's to N's.

   h f x d z m
      i
   _____

   j w s t m u c t
   _____

   d z l k y
   _____

   q m z v z x t
   _____

   m z s t m k f x
            i
   _____

   q r j h f w f t
        i i
   _____

   w k m
   _____

   c l j g
   _____

2. Can you spell four synonyms for the word *permission*? Put one letter in each blank.

   <u>l</u> e <u>a</u> <u>v</u> __
   __ e __ __ __
   __ __ __ e __ e
   __ __ __ __ e __

3. Complete the acrostic puzzle by spelling synonyms for the word *surrender*.

   <u>r</u> <u>e</u> <u>s</u> <u>i</u> <u>g</u> <u>n</u>
         u
   __ __ __ r __ __ __ __
         r
   __ __ e __
         n
   __ __ d __ __ __ __
         e
         r __ __ __ __ __

Name _____

Bonus: Can you spell a pair of rhyming synonyms?

Synonyms Galore

1. To spell seven synonyms for the word *fast*, follow the directions carefully.

   Change the B's to E's.
   Change the G's to A's.
   Change the H's to I's.
   Change the J's to S's.
   Change the Q's to T's.
   Change the V's to M's.
   Change the X's to L's.
   Change the Z's to Y's.

   Leave the other letters as they are.

   r g p h d x z _____

   j p b b d h x z _____

   j w h f q x z _____

   f x b b q x z _____

   h n s t g n q x z _____

   h v v b d h g q b x z _____

   h n j q g n q g n b o u s x z _____

2. Can you spell three synonyms for the word *yearning*? Put one letter in each blank.

   <u>l</u> <u>i</u> <u>k</u> <u>i</u> <u>n</u> <u>g</u>
   __ __ i __ __
   __ __ __ i __
   __ __ __ __ i __

Bonus: To discover four synonyms for the mystery word, unscramble the words found below.

ognrht _____   omb _____

eodrh _____   diuuelmtt _____

Mystery Word: __ __ o __ __

Name _____

Synonym Acrostics

1. Complete this puzzle by spelling synonyms for the word *important*?

   ```
         __ __ i __ __
         __ __ m __ __ __ __ __
   __ __ __ __ __ p __ __
         __ __ __ o __
         __ __ r __ __
   __ __ __ __ __ __ __ __ t __ __ __ __ __
         __ __ __ a __ __ __ __ __
         __ __ __ n __
         __ __ __ __ t __
   ```

2. Complete this puzzle by spelling synonyms for the words *wisdom* and *wise*.

   ```
                w  i  s  e
         __ __ i __ __ __
         __ __ s __ __ __
   __ __ __ __ __ __ __ d __ __
         __ __ o __ __ __ __
         __ m __ __ __
   ```

Name _____

Bonus: Can you spell a nine-letter word containing only one vowel?

__ __ __ __ __ __ __ __ __

More Synonym Acrostics

1. Complete this puzzle by spelling synonyms for the word *agreement*.

    ```
            _ A _ _
          _ _ _ G _ _ _
          _ _ _ R _ _ _
          _ _ _ E _ _ _
            _ E _ _
          _ _ M _ _ _ _
          _ _ E _ _ _
        _ _ N _ _ _ _
      _ _ _ _ _ _ T _ _ _ _ _ _
    ```

2. Complete this puzzle by spelling synonyms for the word *action*.

    ```
      _ _ _ _ A _ _ _ _
      _ _ _ _ C _ _ _ _
        _ _ T _ _ _
        _ _ _ I _ _ _
        _ O _ _ _ _
        _ N _ _ _ _
    ```

Name_____

Bonus: Make your own synonym acrostic using one of your favorite words.

25

Imaginary Synonyms

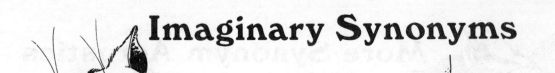

1. Can you spell three synonyms for the word *imaginary*? Each word must begin with the letter *f*.

   f __ __ __ __ __ __
   f __ __ __ __ __ __ __
   f __ __ __ __ __ __ __ __

2. Can you spell four synonyms for the word *conquer*? Each word must begin with the four-letter word *over*.

   over __ __ __ __
   over __ __ __ __ __
   over __ __ __ __ __
   over __ __ __ __

3. Find and circle the two synonyms in each line.

insipid	uninteresting	varied
avid	bored	eager
resilient	brittle	flexible
distinct	obscure	vague
conquest	triumph	failure
alliance	elect	union
quit	endeavor	attempt
exalt	idolize	exit

Name _____

Bonus: Using four vowels, complete this five-letter word that means to stand in line.

q __ __ __ __

Synonym Parts

1. Draw a line to connect word parts to spell synonyms for the word *yell*.

c	wl
c	all
ba	ry
ex	per
h	owl
wh	claim
whim	ine
sh	reech
scr	out
sc	eam
shr	mor
cla	iek
bel	ar
ro	low

Bonus: To discover three synonyms for the mystery word, unscramble the words below.

epryl _____

eorsdpn _____

ttorre _____

Mystery Word: __ __ s w __ __

2. Draw a line to connect word parts that spell synonyms for the word *mix* or *mixture*.

com	use
bl	bine
f	end
min	ge
mer	ion
un	gle
combin	ion
fus	in
jo	ation
com	pound

Name _____

Synonym Scramble

Unscramble the words below and then draw a line to connect the synonyms.

e o o u r s g g
__gorgeous__

l o e u n c c d
_____

e e u i n n g
_____

a i g t n
_____

t t t a a r c
_____

a a e b b f l r g s t
_____

e i o o c f r m s l
_____

a a e i u u n g r t
_____

e i i o d l z
_____

l a r e
_____

t i e e n c
_____

h s i i f n
_____

a a e i v t c r t t
__attractive__

s e o n r m o u
_____

a e o d r
_____

a u f l l p y
_____

a r s t t
_____

e i u r r s s p
_____

Name _____

Bonus: Can you spell a word that contains five *e*'s?
e __ __ e __ __ e __ __ e __ __ e

Synonym Review

1. Can you spell three synonyms for the word *appetizing*? The last letter of each word has been filled in for you.

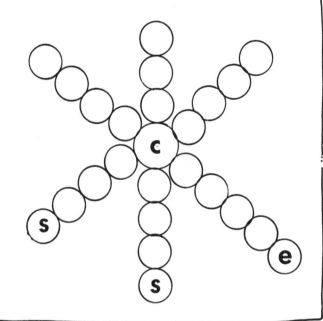

2. Each vowel found in the words below is incorrect. To discover eight synonyms for the word *run*, spell each word with the correct vowels.

   g u̸ l l ø p __gallop__

   l e p o _____

   s p r u n t _____

   j e g _____

   i p u r e t a _____

   i s c u p a _____

   e b s c i n d _____

   f l a u _____

3. One letter in each word found below is incorrect. To discover six synonyms for the word *little*, spell the words with the correct letters. You may need to change the letter more than once.

   s t a l l _____

   b u n y _____

   p e z̸ z̸ y __petty__

   m o n o a t u r e _____

   t r i m i a l _____

   b r a e f _____

Bonus: Can your rearrange the letters in *o, wonder* to spell one word?

Name _____

Antonyms Plenty

1. Can you spell four antonyms for the word *noisy*? The first letter of each word has been filled in for you.

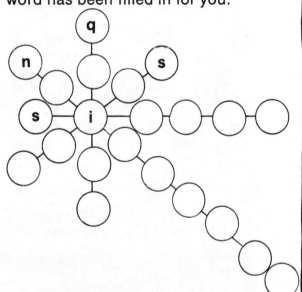

2. Can you spell five antonyms for the word *unpleasant*? Put one letter in each blank and read across.

   __ __ e e __ __
   __ __ e __ __ __ __
   __ __ e e __ __ __ __
   e __ __ __ __ __ __ __ __
   __ e __ __ __ __ __ __ __

3. To solve this puzzle, spell antonyms for each clue given. Words will read across and down.

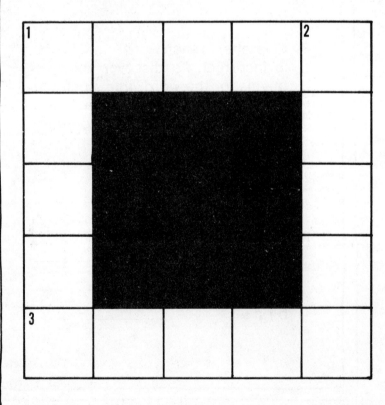

1. → silence
1. ↓ south
2. ↓ loathe
3. → melancholy

Name _____

Bonus: Can you spell a word that contains five *a*'s?
a __ __ a __ a __ a __ __ a

Antonyms Anyone?

1. Unscramble the words below and then draw a line to connect the antonyms.

   g h a u l
   _____laugh_____

   s u i o e r p c
   _____

   c r o e f f u l
   _____

   e e o u r s n g
   _____

   i i a e t t c n r
   _____

   e u b h m l
   _____

   e e a i o c x p t n l
   _____

   e i c f l k

   e s s l h t r w o
   _____

   k w a e
   _____

   h m i w r e p
   _____whimper_____

   g i n s y t
   _____

   o u d r p
   _____

   e i l m s p
   _____

   a o l l y
   _____

   a i o d n r r y

2. Hidden among the letters in each row are two antonyms. Find and circle the two antonyms in each row of letters.

   r e p a i r e a d (b r e a k) e y e s s y
   p e n d a n g e r e d e e r s a f e a r
   b i w e t t i n g d r y e b r e a d m l
   u o h u g e t i n y m b c r e t h i c k

Bonus: What is the longest list of rhyming antonyms you can make? Ten? Twenty? Thirty?

Name _____

Synthetic Antonyms

1. Each row of letters found below is a word without vowels. Add the appropriate vowels as needed to each word to spell four antonyms for the word *graceful*.

   w k w r d
   __awkwa_____

   g w k y
   _____

   b n g l n g
   _____

   c l m s y
   _____

2. Fill in the blanks with consonants to spell two synonyms and two antonyms for the word *symmetrical*.

   __b__ a __l__ a __n__ __ e __
   __ e __ u __ a __
   u __ __ a __ a __ __ e __
   u __ e __ e __

3. Fill in the blanks with vowels to spell two synonyms and two antonyms for the word *synthetic*.

   __a__ r t __i__ f __i__ c __ __ l
   __ m __ t __ t __ __ n
   n __ t __ r __ l
   r __ __ l

4. Can you spell a synonym and an antonym for the word *spread* with the appropriate number of letters to fit in the puzzle found below.

   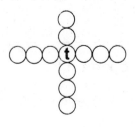

5. Can you spell a synonym and an antonym for the word *fix* with the appropriate number of letters to fit in the puzzle found below?

   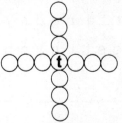

Name _____

Bonus: Can you spell a word beginning with *utm*? An antonym for the mystery word is *least*.

u t m __ __ __

Neat and Rough

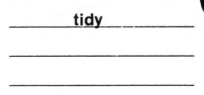

1. Unscramble the synonyms and antonyms for the word *neat*. Put a check by the antonyms for *neat*.

   i t y d   **tidy**

   i o e r l y d d s r   _____

   l e d o r r y   _____

   s s e m y   _____

   l p y p s o   _____

   m t r i   _____

   t d u n i y   _____

   s s p p h h a e i   _____

2. Unscramble the synonyms and antonyms for the word *rough*. Put a check by the antonyms for *rough*.

   a g g e d j   _____

   f s t o   _____

   o r s m t y   _____

   e e v u n n   _____

   v n e e   _____

   g g u r d e   _____

   t h o o m s   _____

   t t h r a i s g   _____

Bonus: Can you spell two synonyms for the word *strong* with the appropriate number of letters to fit in the puzzle?

Name _____

Homonyms, Homonyms

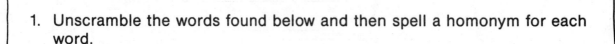

1. Unscramble the words found below and then spell a homonym for each word.

scrambled	word	homonym
e a l n p	**plane**	**plain**
e b l w		
a e u b		
a e u s p		
e e t s w		
a i r f		
o u f l		
l o r l		
a e b s		
a e b k r		
e o d r w		
e d y		

2. Fill in the blanks with consonants to spell four pairs of homonyms.

___ a ___ e   ___ a i ___
___ a ___ e   ___ a i ___
___ a ___ e   ___ a i ___
___ a ___ e   ___ a i ___

Bonus: Choose a pair of homonyms that have the appropriate number of letters to fit in the puzzle found below.

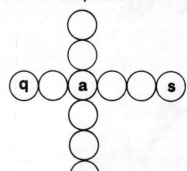

Name _____

More Homonyms

1. Unscramble the words below and then draw a line to connect the homonyms.

   s a e w t _____   l r e w o f _____
   r o l f u _____   e n k w   _____
   w e n   _____   i a t w s   _____
   n n n e a s p t _____   o e w r d   _____
   o u e l s c n _____   n n e a c p _____
   d o a r   _____   o u i c c n l _____

2. If you spell the correct word for each clue given below, you will have written a list of four homonyms.

   to be correct _____
   a ceremony   _____
   to print   _____
   a workman   _____

Bonus: Choose a pair of homonyms that have the appropriate number of letters to fit in the puzzle found below.

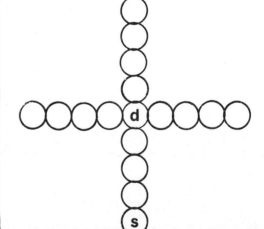

Name _____

35

Animal, Vegetable or Mineral?

Without using a dictionary, how many words can you spell to complete the chart found below. After you try without your dictionary, then complete as much of the chart as you can using your dictionary. There are many different answers, but there aren't answers for some of the spaces.

	Animal	Vegetable (plants)	Mineral (elements)
a	aardvark		
b			boron
c			
d			
e			erbium
f			
g			
h			
i			
j			
k		kiwi	
l			
m			
n			
o			
p			
q			
r		rutabaga	
s			
t			
u			
v			
w			
x			
y			
z			

Name_____

Whatch-A-Ma-Call-Its

1. Unscramble the words in the first column. Then draw a line connecting the words with the appropriate clue.

   a e e i r **aerie** — small organisms
   e f z _____ eagle's nest
   a a e c r h j k m m _____ rock drill
   a o l k n n p t _____ hat
   o u p l _____ a window
   a a f g h n _____ doily for a chair
   e o d m r r _____ crocheted blanket
   a a a a i n t m c s s r _____ leap

2. Find and circle the names of thirteen endangered species hidden in the letter maze.

   ```
   G O R I L L A E A G L E
   W A W F E R R E T P O E
   O B Z H F O X A B O X C
   L I S E A B C O N D O R
   F R D W L L I D O G C A
   F A C A N L E S O S T N
   R H I N O C E R O S T E
   X C O U G A R O R N S A
   W O O D P E C K E R E T
   ```

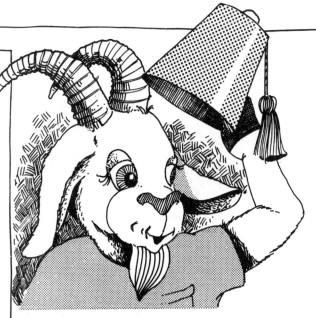

Name _____

Bonus: Complete this six-letter word that means to drink.

__ __ z z __ __

37

Mind Bogglers

There are special names for groups of animals. Unscramble the words found below. Then draw a line to connect the animal and the appropriate group.

i c h c k e n	chicken	o l c o n y	_____
e h s p e	_____	e v h i	_____
e b e	_____	d o o b r	_____
s i f h	_____	a b n d	_____
n a t	_____	o r d v e	_____
e s g o o	_____	l e a g g	_____
i r g o l l a	_____	o o c s h l	_____
r h s o e	_____	m a t e	_____
f l w o	_____	v b e y	_____
a i l q u	_____	r s m u t e	_____
e l m u	_____	e r p i d	_____
k n m o e y	_____	d o p	_____
a b e r	_____	p r t o o	_____
l h w a e	_____	h e s l u t	_____
n o l i	_____	p s a n	_____
c a p e c o k	_____	c p a k	_____

Name _____

Bonus: Use the animals you listed as clues to a crossword puzzle. The group names will be the fill-in words.

38

More Bogglers

1. Give each letter of the alphabet a number. Example a = 1, b = 2, c = 3, etc.
   _____
   _____

2. What are the most points you can get for a five-letter word? ____

   Example: Xerox = 24 + 5 + 18 + 15 + 24 = 86 points.

3. What are the least points you can get for a five-letter word? ____

   Example: bagel = 2 + 1 + 7 + 5 + 12 = 27 points.

Name_____

Bonus: What are the most points you can get for a word containing as many letters as you choose? ____ What is the word? _____

It Can Be Done!

2. Write a sentence of at least ten words with as few letters as possible.

   Example: I am I, he is he, and we are we. = 21 letters

3. The answers to the clues below are words that begin with the same three letters.

   a machine for weaving _____

   a fish-eating bird _____

   a small narrow opening _____

4. What do the words found below have in common?

   gnat   knee

   knob   sign

   _____

1. Find and circle the misspelled word in each sentence. Write the misspelled word correctly on the blank after each sentence.

   "Horse and raspy," describes a harsh sounding voice.

   _____

   The impish and mischeivous kitten batted the ball of yarn around the kitchen.

   _____

   The wheather was hot, humid and damp.

   _____

   A miniature means some thing that is scaled down or reduced in size.

   _____

   Why do you worry about something as trivial as a broken finger nail?

   _____

   There was a brief paws when our conversation began.

   _____

Bonus: Many words have multiple meanings. Can you spell a word that fits all four of the clues listed below?

___ ___ ___ ___

a type of bird
to brag
a bar or iron with a claw
to make a loud shrill sound

Name _____

Hide and Seek Spelling

1. Can you spell one word that fits both word clues found in each line below?

    enclosure, three feet ____**yard**____

    marvel, doubt _____

    labor, operate _____

    void, clean _____

    educate, railroad _____

    jump, omit _____

    lake, combine _____

    sound, circle _____

    child, joke _____

2. Hidden in the letter maze are ten parts of the body. The words may be written in a straight line or have one curve. You must circle every letter once.

    ```
    h e a r e a r
    l s t t t o e
    u n o m a c h
    n o s e b r a
    g s k n e e i
    s k e l e s n
    e y e s t o n
    m u s c l e s
    ```

3. Each sentence found below needs two words. The words you add must rhyme and one of them must begin with the letter *t*.

    He is very _____,

    bigger than _____.

    There is an _____ to

    baking a _____.

    She will do a _____

    if you only _____

Name _____

Bonus: Can you spell the name of an animal that contains the letter *z* and double *l*'s?

You Decide

1. Some words end and begin with the same letters. Fill in the beginning and ending for each word with the same letters.

   Example: __ __ g __ __ = <u>e</u> d g e d

   __ __ e r n e __ __   __ __ t a b l i s h __ __
   __ __ r i __   __ __ a d a b __ __
   __ __ s e n c __ __   __ __ a t __ __
   __ __ e l l f i __ __   __ __ o t o g r a __ __
   __ __ s u l __ __   __ __ r a n g e __ __
   __ __ o n o g r a __ __   __ __ a s __ __

2. Use all the letters found below to spell three animals.

   d e g g g i
   o o o p s

   _____
   _____
   _____

3. Use all the letters found below to spell three vegetables.

   a b e e i
   n n o o o
   m o t t t

   _____
   _____
   _____

   Name _____

Bonus: What eleven-letter word ends and begins with *ing*?
_____

Weeding Words

1. Cross out the correct seven letters found below and you will be left with a famous saying.

   a d d p e n n y o u s a v e d i
   s a n p e x n n y b e a r n e d

   _____
   _____

2. Cross out the extra vowels in the sentences found below and you will be left with three sentences that make sense. Then rewrite the sentences with spaces between the words.

   A l o a t o f e l e a t t e r s
   c a n e b e a f o u n d a t e t
   h e p o a s t o f f i u c e.

   A lot_____
   _____

   A e g o o d e p e u a z z l e
   a i s a o n e i t h a t e m e
   a k e s y o u t h i e n k e.

   _____
   _____

   T h e a p r i o u z e w a i s
   w o n e b y e a e w e e a l a
   e d n a i m e d E a d i.

   _____
   _____

3. Some words have more than one set of double letters. Double some of the letters in each series of letters found below to form words.

   a c e s i b i l i t y
   _____

   e m b a r a s m e n t
   _____

   b a l o n
   _____

   o c a s i o n a l y
   _____

   b o k e p e r
   _____

   Name _____

Bonus: Can you spell two animals that have the same double letters?

Can You Spell?

1. How many words can you spell using only the first seven letters of the alphabet? Can you spell ten? Twenty?

   aba

2. Can you spell twenty-four word pairs that have the same letters except one has the vowel *i* and the other has the vowel *a*?

   Example: big & bag

   _____ & _____

Bonus: Make a list of words using only the last six letters of the alphabet.

Name _____

Eight Great ATEs

Answer each question found below with a word that rhymes with *ate*.

1. Who never ATE alone? _____

2. Who ATE with his boss? _____

3. Who ATE happily? _____

4. Who ATE like everyone else? _____

5. Who disappeared when he ATE? _____

6. Who ATE alone? _____

7. Who ATE for a vote? _____

8. Who ATE later? _____

Name _____

Bonus: Can you add seven letters to the word *men* and spell something very basic? __ __ __ __ __ __ __ __ __ __

Word Chains

1. A word chain is formed by changing one letter of a word several times to create a new word. Each time a letter is changed, a new word must be spelled. Complete these word chains.

   c a k e
   <u>l</u> <u>a</u> <u>k</u> <u>e</u>
   _ _ _ _
   f a c e

   c h a p
   _ _ _ _
   _ _ _ _
   _ _ _ _
   s h o e

   h e a d
   _ _ _ _
   _ _ _ _
   _ _ _ _
   f e e t

Name _____

2. Write any three-letter word. Drop the first letter and add a letter at the end of the two remaining letters to form a new word. Repeat this process as many times as you can. What is the longest chain of words that you can make? You may not repeat a word in the chain.

   Example: the, her, era, rap, ape, pea, eat, ate, tea, ear, art . . .

Bonus: Write any four-letter word. Drop the first letter and add a letter at the end of the three remaining letters to form a new word. What is the longest chain of four-letter words you can make?

46

More Word Chains

Name _____

To complete the word chains found below, drop one letter at a time, always leaving a word until you end the word chain with a one-letter word at the bottom of the chain.

b r a n d y
b ~~r~~ **a n d**
b a n d
_ _ _
_ _
_

c r a t e r s
_ _ _ _ _ _
_ _ _ _ _
_ _ _ _
_ _ _
_ _
_

p i r a t e d
_ _ _ _ _ _
_ _ _ _ _
_ _ _ _
_ _ _
_ _
_

t r a m p s
_ _ _ _ _
_ _ _ _
_ _ _
_ _
_

Bonus: To discover four clues to the mystery word, unscramble the words found below.

m o a m c _____   r o o a e p p s t h _____

c o o n l _____   p h h e n y _____

Mystery Word: _ _ _ _ _ _ _ u a _ _ _ _

47

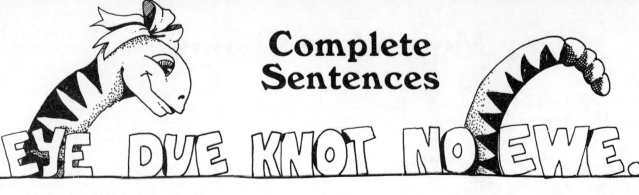

Complete Sentences

1. What is the longest sentence you can write in which every word has the vowel *e*? Example: June gave me her red hen yesterday.

2. Write a short story in which every word contains the vowel *a*.

3. What is the longest sentence you can write in which every word is a homonym for what you mean? Example: Eye due knot no ewe.

4. Can you think of a sentence that contains all twenty-six letters of the alphabet? Example: The quick brown fox jumps over the lazy dog.

Bonus: How many five-letter words can you list that are spelled in alphabetical order? Example: adept

Name _____

More Mystery Word Fun

How many words can you spell, moving from square to square? You may move one square at a time horizontally, vertically or diagonally. Can you spell fifteen? Twenty? Thirty?

Name _____

Bonus: Create your own 5" x 5" puzzle square. Place one letter of the alphabet, except letter *z*, in each square. You may place the letters in any order. Think of combinations that will spell as many words as possible. What are the most words you can spell using your puzzle?

Perfect Word Squares

1. Using the five clues given, complete the word square. The words must read the same down as well as across.

   1. vital organ
   2. weird
   3. got up
   4. elevated
   5. older children

	1.	2.	3.	4.	5.
1.	h	e	a	r	t
2.	e				
3.	a				
4.	r				
5.	t				

2. Using the five clues given, complete the word square. The words must read the same down as well as across.

   1. squander
   2. entertainer
   3. rock
   4. medicine
   5. upright

Bonus: Create your own perfect word square. Give the clues below, and see if your friend can solve your puzzle.

Name _____

Mystery Word Magic

1. To discover clues to the mystery word, complete each word below.

    <u>T</u> <u>o</u> <u>m</u> ato

    __ __ __ hine

    __ __ __ ple

    __ __ __ id

    __ __ __ __ h

    __ __ __ key

    __ __ __ __ __ le

    __ __ __ __ __ furter

    Mystery Word: __ __ __ __

2. To discover the mystery word, find and circle twelve related words hidden in the letter maze. The twelve related words you circle will give you clues to the mystery word.

    ```
    b s l i n g u i s t
    i p x d w o r d w o
    l e l i n g o r d s
    i e x a j a r g o n
    n c a l p h a b e t
    g h l e c i p h e r
    u t e c v o w e l r
    a t e t s p e l l s
    l c o n s o n a n t
    ```

    Mystery Word:
    __ a __ __ __ a __ __

Name _____

Bonus: Cross out the right letters in the row of letters found below, and you will be left with the mystery word.   p̶h̶y̶s̶i̶y̶e̶s̶c̶t̶h̶i̶c̶
Mystery Word: __ __ __ __ __

Ten-Letter Words

ABLE TO DO SOMETHING

1. To discover four meanings of the mystery word, put spaces between the words in each row of letters found below to form phrases. Each phrase is a different meaning for the mystery word.

   a b l e | t o | d o s o m e t h i n g
   able to _____

   v e s s e l f o r h o l d i n g l i q u i d s
   _____

   t o p r e s e r v e b y s e a l i n g
   _____

   t o d i s c h a r g e o r d i s m i s s
   _____

   Mystery Word: ___ ___ ___

2. To discover the mystery words, find and circle a ten-letter word in each row of letters found below. The uncircled letters will spell the mystery words.

   s u s p i n d i g e n o u s
   e n i n f a l l i b l e s i
   i n o r d i n a t e o n b r
   i c h i m p a n z e e d g e

   Mystery Words: _ _ _ _ _ _ _ _ _ _ _ _ _ _ _

Name _____

Bonus: Add the same two letters to the beginnings of the two words found below and you will have written synonyms for the mystery word.

   ___ ___ a i l
   ___ ___ a g i l e
   Mystery Word: ___ ___ ___ k

52

Mystery Word Zoo

1. To discover clues to the mystery word, put a vowel in each blank to form words.

   c __ l t
   f __ w n
   f __ l l y
   g __ s l __ n g
   h __ __ f __ r
   j __ __ y
   k __ d
   k __ t
   s q __ __ b
   y __ __ r l __ n g

   Mystery Word: __ __ b __ __ __

Name _____

2. To discover clues to the mystery word, put spaces between the words in each row of letters found below.

   t o d a s h o r s p l a s h
   _____

   a s u d d e n f l a m e
   _____

   p a s s v e r y q u i c k l y
   _____

   d i s p l a y i n a s h o w y m a n n e r
   _____

   Mystery Word: __ __ __ __

3. To discover clues to the mystery word, put a vowel in each blank to form words.

   l __ v __ l y

   p __ p p y

   s p __ r __ t __ d

   __ g __ l __

   __ n __ r g __ t __ c

   Mystery Word: __ __ __ __ __ __

Bonus: What four-letter word means to wish, desire, crave and need?

__ __ __ __

Palindromes

1. A palindrome is a word that is spelled the same frontwards as well as backwards. *Mom* is an example of a palindrome. To discover a clue for each palindrome, unscramble the words.

   l a t n o z i r o h

   <u>horizontal</u> __ __ v __ __

   c p i i t h s n e z i

   _____ __ __ v __ __

   r e t c i d

   _____ __ __ f __ __

   o j e k

   _____ __ a __

   t h r e a f

   _____ __ a __

2. Complete each sentence found below with a palindrome.

   I will invite my mom and __ __ __.

   We will leave at __ __ __ __.

   __ __ __ you know her?

   I think she __ __ __ __ you.

   He played a __ __ __ on Jack.

   She bought the baby a __ __ __.

   I will name my dog __ __ __.

   Please buy me a bottle of __ __ __.

   I enjoy doing a good __ __ __ __.

   __ __ __! This tastes great?

Name _____

Bonus: Write a sentence, with five or more words, that is a PALINDROME.
Example: Was it a cat I saw?

Spelling Puns

1. A pun is a humorous use of words which have the same sound or spelling, but have different meanings. Think of a "punny" response for each statement found below.

   Spell a good drink for a boxer. _____

   Spell a good dessert for a shoemaker. _____

   Spell a good cloth for a banker to wear. _____

   Spell a good cloth for a dairyman to wear. _____

   Spell a good name for a dancer. _____

   Spell a good name for a porter. _____

   Spell a good name for a happy girl. _____

2. Answer each question found below using a word that sounds like a number or has a number sound in the word.

   Who is the victor? _____

   What is your middle name? _____

   What did the cowboy call the city boy? _____

   What happened to the cake? _____

Bonus: The mystery word is what someone might call you now that you have completed this page.

Mystery Word: __ __ __ s __ __ __

Name _____

Answer Key

Word Wheels Page 1
1. sun, fun, man, fan, ton, son, den, pen
2. big, dig, wag, bag, bug, dug, leg, beg
3. paw, saw, now, bow, sew, new, how, cow
4. did, hid, pod, nod, bad, had, fed, bed

Word Diamonds Page 2
1. bad, makes, ten, bat, cakes, den
2. bib, bakes, get, bag, likes, bet

Little Words Page 3
1. speak, party, boils, brats, thumb, brand, spine, trank, honey
2. thorns, tramps, treads, crusts

Bonus: rhythm

Something's Missing Page 4
1. ant: chant, gallant, grant, scant, plant
2. rim, brink, Pacific, outline
3. file, hammer, vise, pliers, drill, scissors, protractor, screwdriver
4. lever, wheel, pulley, derrick, fulcrum, rudder, crowbar, wedge

Fill-Ins Page 5
1. current, new, modern, recent, young
2. get, event, receive, bequeath
3. balloon, bubble, biggest
4. ar: guitar, caviar, star

Bonus: part

Missing Consonants and Vowels Page 6
1. To have friends, be a friend.
   You can learn from every person you meet.
   Like yourself and others will like you too.
2. The time to be happy is now.
   A happy friend is like a jolly song

Bonus: A day of the week

Safe Additives Page 7
I need a spoon to eat my pudding.
She is too wee to reach the fiddle.
A rabbit ran across the grass too fast to see.
A ball will roll downhill.
Three trees will freeze when sleet falls.

Bonus: somersault

Add Two or Three Page 8
1. Bev, Fran, Jo, May, Kitty, Pat, Chris, Liz
2. claw, chew, chow, crow, crew
3. aff: staff, giraffe, chaff
4. cat, pig, cow, bug, fly, ape, bee

Bonus: They are all misspelled.

S.W. and S.T.R. Page 9
1. swoop, swirl, swerve, swag, swagger, swap, swarm, swash, sway, swing, sweep, swish, swim
2. straddle, straggle, straightaway, strand, stroke, stray, strenuous, stress, stretch, strew, stride, strive, strife, stroll, strike, strow, struck, struggle, strut

Bonus: delightful

Vowels and Consonants Needed Page 10
1. keep the ball rolling,
   through thick and thin,
   whole kit and caboodle,
   paint the town red,
   in the nick of time,
   know the ropes,
   out on a limb,
2. horse of another color,
   an ax to grind,
   rain cats and dogs,
   upset the apple cart,
   to talk turkey,
   let the cat out of the bag

Bonus: llama

Alphabet Sentences Page 11
Answers will vary.

Missing and Extra Letters Page 12
1. Adam said Hi madam.
   Bill plays baseball.
   Tiny Tim can tie knots.
   Allen ate an orange.
2. It is too late to see the movie.
   I saw a bug on the flower.
   Here today, gone tomorrow.
3. vehicle, dazzled, dolphin, goulash

Great, Grand and Clue Page 13
1. ate, bait, crate, date, eight, fate gate, hate, irate, late, mate, nominate, plate, rate, skate, trait, violate, wait
2. gland, grand, command, withstand, understand, expand
3. adieu, askew, debut, interview

Bonus: reprimand

Day and Grade Page 14
1. array, away, bay, bray, clay, convey, betray, bouquet, croquet, decay, delay, dismay, display, essay, gay, gray, jay, lay, may, matinee, mislay, obey, pay, slay, portray, pray, protege, prey, say, relay, repay, sachet, say, slay, sleigh, spray, stay, stray, survey, sway, way, weigh
2. stockade, arcade, tirade, marmalade, cascade, masquerade, suede, charade

Dynamite and Giraffes Page 15
1. appetite, bite, blight, bright, contrite, delight, despite, excite, expedite, fight, fright, height, ignite, invite, kite, knight, light, might, night, oversight, parasite, plight, polite, quite, recite, right, satellite, sight, slight, spite, sprite, tight, tonight, unite, white, write
2. photograph, paragraph, phonograph, telegraph

Bonus: Orange

Lightweight Rhymes Page 16
1. ounce: flounce, bounce, pounce, announce, pronounce
2. black, clack, crack, knack, quack, snack, stack, track, whack
3. spice, price, slice, dice, twice, rice, advice, lice

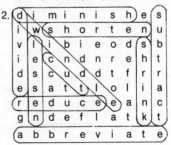

Rhyme Time Page 17
1. horoscope, heliotrope, antelope
2. cartoon, typhoon, balloon
3. critique, meek, bleak, cheek, leek, seek, antique
4. faint, paint, quaint, acquaint, saint, complaint, constraint, restraint

Synonym Search Page 18
1. tool, implement, device, utensil, appliance
2. mark, speck, smudge, stain, blotch, blot, blemish
3. foresee, forecast, foretell, forewarn

Bonus: Egyptian, solid figure, sloping sides
Mystery Word: pyramid

Synonyms, Synonyms Page 19
1. bloom, rule, is, male
2. same, identical; show, display; sleep, rest
3. tether, integrity, baffle, rout, fracture, valor, exalt, imitation

Synonym Roundup Page 20
1. roam, ramble, meander, drift, stray

3. stable, steady

Bonus: think, consider

Answer Key

Synonym Puzzles Page 21
1. recreation, fun, delight, entertainment, interest
2. radiant, lustrous, sparkling, twinkling, glimmering (or gleaming)
3. inquiry, investigation, probe, scrutiny, examination, check-up

Bonus: rock

Synonyms, Please Page 22
1. hinder, obstruct, delay, prevent, restrain, prohibit, bar, clog
2. leave, permit, license, consent
3. resign, sacrifice, yield, abdicate, renounce

Bonus: expose, disclose

Synonyms Galore Page 23
1. rapidly, speedily, swiftly, fleetly, instantly, immediately, instantaneously
2. liking, thirst, desire, longing (or craving)

Mystery Word: crowd: throng, mob, horde, multitude

Synonym Acrostics Page 24
1. chief, momentous, principal, major, great, significant, leading, main, mighty
2. wise, insight, sensible, levelheaded, reasonable, smart

Bonus: strengths

More Synonym Acrostics Page 25
1. pact, bargain, approval, treaty, deal, compact, pledge, contract, understanding
2. operation, exercise, motion, activity, process, conduct

Imaginary Synonyms Page 26
1. fanciful, fantastic, fictitious
2. overcome, overthrow, overpower, overwhelm
3. insipid, uninteresting
   avid, eager;
   resilient, flexible;
   obscure, vague;
   conquest, triumph
   alliance, union
   endeavor, attempt;
   exalt, idolize

Bonus: queue

Synonym Parts Page 27
1. call, cry, bawl, exclaim, howl, whine, whimper, shout, scream, screech, shriek, clamor, bellow, roar
2. combine, blend, fuse, mingle, merge, union, combination, fusion, join, compound

Bonus: reply, respond, retort
Mystery Word: answer

Synonym Scramble Page 28
gorgeous, attractive;
conclude, finish;
genuine, real;
giant, enormous;
attract, entice;
flabbergast, surprise;
frolicsome, playful;
inaugurate, start;
idolize, adore

Bonus: effervescence

Synonym Review Page 29
1. luscious, delectable, delicious
2. gallop, lope, sprint, jog, operate, escape, abscond, flee
3. small, puny, petty, miniature, trivial, brief

Bonus: one word

Antonyms Plenty Page 30
1. silent, noiseless, quiet, still
2. cheery, pleasing, cheerful, enchanting, delightful
3. noise
   o   n
   r   j
   t   o
   happy

Bonus: abracadabra

Antonyms Anyone? Page 31
1. laugh, whimper;
   precious, worthless
   forceful, weak;
   generous, stingy;
   intricate, simple;
   humble, proud;
   exceptional, ordinary
   fickle, loyal;
2. repair, break;
   endangered, safe;
   wet, dry;
   huge, tiny

Synthetic Antonyms Page 32
1. awkward, gawky, bungling, clumsy
2. balanced, regular, unbalanced, uneven
3. artificial, imitation, natural, real
4. scatter, gather
5. restore, destroy

Bonus: utmost

Neat and Rough Page 33
1. tidy, disorderly✓, orderly, messy✓, sloppy✓, trim, untidy✓, shipshape
2. jagged, soft✓, stormy, uneven, even✓, rugged, smooth✓, straight✓

Bonus: powerful, sturdy

Homonyms, Homonyms Page 34
1. plane, plain; blew, blue; beau, bow; pause, paws; sweet, suite; fair, fare; foul, fowl; roll, role; base, bass; brake, break; rowed, road, dye, die
2. bale, bail, pale, pail, tale, tail, sale, sail (Accept any correct answer.)

Bonus: quarts, quartz

More Homonyms Page 35
1. waste, waist; flour, flower; new, knew, pennants, penance; counsel, council; road, rowed;
2. right, rite, write, wright

Bonus: incidence, incidents

Animal, Vegetable or Mineral? Page 36
aardvark, artichoke, aluminum
bear, bean, boron
cat, carrot, copper
dog, dandelion, dysprosium
elephant, eggplant, erbium
frog, fennel, fluorine
goat, greens, gold
hen, huckleberry, helium
iguana, iris, iron
kangaroo, kale, krypton
lion, lettuce, lead
monkey, mushroom, mercury
nag, navy bean, nickel
opossum, okra, oxygen
porcupine, parsnip, platinum
quail, quince, quartz
rabbit, rutabaga, radium
snake, squash, silver
turtle, tomato, tin
unicorn, udo, uranium
vulture, vanilla, vanadium
yak, yam, yttrium
zebra, zucchini, zinc

Whatch-A-Ma-Call-Its Page 37
1. aerie, eagle's nest;
   fez, hat;
   jackhammer, rock drill;
   plankton, small organisms;
   loup, leap;
   afghan, crocheted blanket;
   dormer, a window;
   antimacassar, doily for a chair

2. Word search with: GORILLA, EAGLE, FERRET, FOX, CONDOR, DOG, RHINOCEROS, COUGAR, WOODPECKER

Bonus: guzzle

Mind Bogglers Page 38
chicken, brood; sheep, drove; bee, hive; fish, school; ant, colony; goose, gaggle; gorilla, band; horse, team; wolf, pack; quail, bevy; mule, span; monkey, troop; bear, sleuth; whale, pod; lion, pride; peacock, muster

Answer Key

More Bogglers Page 39
Answers will vary.

It Can Be Done! Page 40
1. horse (hoarse), mischeivous (mischievous), wheather (weather), some thing (something), finger nail (fingernail), paws (pause)
2. Answers will vary.
3. loom, loon, loop
4. They all have a silent consonant.

Bonus: crow

Hide and Seek Spelling Page 41
1. yard, wonder, work, vacuum, train, skip, pool, ring, kid

2.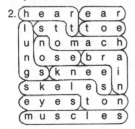

3. tall, all; art, tart; task, ask

Bonus: gazelle

You Decide Page 42
1. sternest, deride, essences, shellfish, insulin, phonograph, establishes, leadable, orator, photograph strangest, eraser
2. dog, pig, goose
3. onion, beet, tomato

Bonus: ingathering

Weeding Words Page 43
1. A penny saved is a penny earned.
2. A lot of letters can be found at the post office.
   A good puzzle is one that makes you think.
   The prize was won by a wee lad named Ed.
3. accessibility, embarrassment, balloon, occasionally, bookkeeper

Bonus: llama, gazelle

Can You Spell? Page 44
1. abaca, bee, cabbage, gage, gag, cafe, beg, bed, cab, fed, fad, gad, ace, face, dab, gab, bad, bead, bag, fade, bade, badge, cage, deaf
2. chip, chap; clip, clap; flip, flap; lip, lap; nip, nap; scrip, scrap; sip, sap; big, bag; jig, jag; rig, rag; snick, snack; slip, slap; snip, snap; tip, tap; trip, trap; strip, strap; fire, fare; hire, hare; shire, share; spire, spare; wire, ware; did, dad; hid, had; lid, lad; ice, ace; lice, lace; rice, race; spice, space; vise, vase; pick, pack

Eight Great ATEs Page 45
1. cooperate or participate
2. subordinate
3. celebrate
4. emulate or imitate
5. evaporate
6. separate
7. candidate
8. procrastinate

Bonus: elementary

Word Chains Page 46
1. cake, lake, lace, face
   chap, chip, ship, shop, shoe
   head, heat, seat, meat, meet, feet

More Word Chains Page 47
brandy, brand, band, ban, an, a
craters, crater, crate, rate, rat, at, a
pirated, pirate, irate, rate, ate, or rat, at, a
tramps, ramps, ramp, ram, am, a

Bonus: comma, colon, apostrophe, hyphen
Mystery Word: punctuation

Complete Sentences Page 48
Answers will vary.

More Mystery Word Fun Page 49
bad, back, bat, bead, beat, bet, bid, bin, cab, cabin, cafe, cat, dad, date, dim, din, face, fact, fat, feat, flea, go, golf, got, he, head, heat, jab, lead, leaf, let, mid, mind, numb, pin, so, stole, tea, toe, to, wheat

Perfect Word Squares Page 50
1. heart   2. waste
   eerie   actor
   arose   stone
   risen   tonic
   teens   erect

Mystery Word Magic Page 51
1. tomato, machine, sample, timid, dough, donkey, chuckle, frankfurter
Mystery Word: boys

2. [word search grid with words: linguist, word, lingo, words, jargon, alphabet, cipher, vowel, spells, consonant]

Mystery Word: language
Bonus: psychic

Ten-Letter Words Page 52
1. able to do something
   vessel for holding liquids
   to preserve by sealing
   to discharge or dismiss
Mystery Word: can
2. indigenous, infallible, inordinate, chimpanzee
Mystery Words: suspension bridge
Bonus: frail, fragile
Mystery Word: weak

Mystery Word Zoo Page 53
1. colt, fawn, filly, gosling, heifer, joey, kid, kit, squab, yearling
Mystery Word: babies
2. to dash or splash
   a sudden flame
   pass very quickly
   display in a showy manner
Mystery Word: flash
3. lively, peppy, spirited, agile, energetic
Mystery Word: active
Bonus: want

Palindromes Page 54
1. horizontal, level; citizenship, civic; direct, refer; joke, gag; father, dad
2. dad, noon, did, sees, gag, bib, Bob, pop, deed, Wow

Spelling Puns Page 55
1. punch, cobbler, cashmere, cheesecloth, Grace, Carrie, Mary
2. The one who won.
   I forgot.
   tenderfoot
   He ate it.
Bonus: punster

Bonus Award Certificate

To _____

From _____

Expert Word Builder

To _____   From _____

_____

Super Speller!

To _____
_____
From _____
_____

Synonym Champ

To _____

From _____

Mystery Word Award

To _____
From _____

Congratulations!